Hope Station USA

Brandi Payne

This is a work of fiction. Similarities to real people, places, or events are entirely coincidental.

Hope Station USA

First edition. May 2, 2019.

Copyright © 2019 Brandi Payne.

Written by Brandi Payne.

Dedication

First, I want to dedicate this book to my loving and caring husband, Clifford. I love you, honey. Secondly, I want to recognize Richard Palmer for being very supportive of my dream. Thank you, Rick. Then, I want to dedicate this book to Tammy Dollinger who I know is sitting in Heaven watching down over us. I miss you Tammy. Lastly, I want to dedicate this book to every person who has been homeless once in their life and came out of it a champion. To those still out there surviving, I am fighting for your self-sufficiency.

THE IDEA

There are many people in the world with many ideas and how many of those ideas are put into motion? An idea can be anything from a new toy to a new car style, but what about an idea to help people? I am talking about the people who live under bridges and those who pull food from the dumpsters just to eat. I am not sure how homelessness began, but I want to help end it which is a far reach for just one person. The saying is that it only takes one person to change the world and I mean to try.

The people living out in the streets are just like you and I, except they fell on hard times which they could not recover from. Losing everything because you lost your job or income can be devastating to any person. Seeing these people struggle to survive is heart wrenching for me. I know because I was once out there with them.

I ran away from home at an early age only to find myself homeless and with no money in my pocket. I struggled every day to try and make a few dollars to buy food to eat and what personal hygiene products I might have needed at the time. It took me a few years to catch on to what being homeless meant and the day to day activities it took to survive.

After making the mistake of leaving home and knowing that I disappointed everyone in my family because of a wrong choice that I made, I was filled with guilt and shame and that is when I found out what drugs were. My drug of choice was crack cocaine and when getting high it numbed all those feelings up to where I could function and focus on what I needed to do next to survive and keep moving forward.

Any traumatic event at home can cause someone to fall into the trap of drugs or alcohol abuse just to cope with the situation they are faced with. I have seen people lose a loved one and find solace in drugs or alcohol.

I spent twenty-three years homeless living on the streets because I got sucked into the downward spiral of the whirlpool with my hand outstretched for someone to help, but there was no one there to help me. It seemed like the more I kicked and came up for air, the further down I was going each time. It didn't stop me, and I just kept swimming up to try and make it out of the nightmare I was in.

Back in two-thousand and eight, I did one more trip to jail and the whole ninety days that I sat in there, I thought about what life meant to me. I wanted to live and was in fear of being sent back into the wilderness with the wolves who were just waiting for you to falter. I had intentions of staying away from the streets and my husband at the time rescued me and kept me away from going back.

I ended up getting a job and working a normal one which gave me a way to pay for things that I needed. I was happy about my situation, but then the thought hit me about those who were still out there fighting for their lives. Seeing the news, one homeless person was beaten to death by some young kids who were making fun of him for being homeless. It was such a shame that even the youth today see a homeless individual as a piece of trash that they can do whatever they want to them and get away with it. Society just looked at it as one less panhandler bothering them for change, but it was still a human being.

So, sitting on the front porch with my husband at the time, I reminisced about being out there and the people I met from all walks of life. I missed some of them dearly because they took me in when I was younger and looked after me like I was one of their children. They did most of the money making and food searches to keep me out of trouble and to keep me close from being taken advantage of by some of the others who had mental illnesses and were not responsible for their own actions.

Sometimes I wonder what has happened to these individuals after I left. Are they still alive? Are they still living on the streets? Even when I was out there, I still had a heart for people. Not everyone out there was a bad person and most of them will look out for one another. There were those who stayed to themselves and kept out of the drama, but still managed to get included into it when there were repercussions following arguments. They were innocent bystanders who got caught up in the drama.

After doing my time in jail for the last time back in two-thousand and eight, I thought about how I could best use my talents and compassion to help everyone I could that was still living on the streets. It is like it pulled on my heart strings every time I saw someone pushing a shopping cart with everything they own in it, or asleep in the bushes. I wanted to help but was unsure of how to do that.

I am no better than anyone out there except that I have a place safe to lay my head and that is what I wanted for all of them especially during the colder months. Seeing people sleep on cold sidewalks with people just walking around them is hard to imagine but it is a reality that we must share.

I needed a way to help them get back into society, but I had no knowledge of where to start. I sat with a notebook one day and jotted down notes of what things I could do to help them. I could feed and give them old clothes I had, but most places do that already. I could use my laptop and help them apply for jobs and allow them to use my address, not many people were doing that. I could give them some advice and recommendations on how to help themselves and only a few places did that by giving them a piece of paper with other places to go.

I needed something unique that could cause a trend with other organizations, but that would be a little difficult seeing that most of them just feed or give them a bag of food and send them on their way. To me it would be personal a bit because I want to know everyone and make sure they know me and can come to me even if they just need someone to talk to. What could I do?

Then, the idea finally hit me. I wanted a place where they could come every day and get food to eat, clothing, hygiene products, a job or income, plus I wanted to give them some hope, hope for a brighter future. Most of them needed that because being out on the streets beats you down every day that you are out there. Your self-esteem is knocked so low and eventually you have no more hope and are only going through the motions like a zombie.

The name then came as quick as the idea and it summed up everything I wanted them to have and that was "Hope Station USA". It would be a place for them to not only get the items needed, but they would leave with hope that things would get better.

Once the idea hit me, it was now time to figure out how to get things going or at least get it started in the right direction. I had my notebook and it was almost like daydreaming writing all the things down that I wanted to provide them with and ideas of how to help them. The list became a long one as I brainstormed.

Once the list was pretty much exhausted from my mind, I had to narrow it down and prioritize what was most important to have in a service and then the rest would follow. I now had my list ready and prioritized and the next step was to find out how to get the things I needed to help them as fast as I could.

My husband at the time was very supportive and once I brought this to his attention, he wanted to do everything he could to help me.

One of the first things we did was take some of our money and went to the grocery store. We bought the items needed to make hearty bag lunches and loaded them up in a borrowed shopping cart. We pushed that shopping cart around town and passed out bag lunches to everyone that was homeless or hungry.

It was surprising to see the appreciation we received from everyone who got something to eat. We heard a "thank you" or "God bless" with every lunch we handed out. Once we were done and all the lunches were passed out, we headed back towards the house and talked about how each of us felt and how things went and how we could get things going legally. I say legally because in certain cities, they have banned public feeding of the homeless.

Once we made it back to the house and cleaned up the mess, we made from making the bag lunches, we sat and communicated our ideas to one another and threw out ideas of what we should or could do. I loved the fact that he was very supportive. I was pleased with what we did, and it was satisfying to know that we did help some people.

The next thing to do was find out how to go about making it legal and then being able to pull in the funding needed to help more and be able to buy more supplies. I sat and thought about it for a while and listened to some suggestions from my husband and some other business people that I knew. It was time to do some research.

THE RESEARCH

About a week later, I found myself needing to go to the public library to look up some things and then my research would begin. I found out that in order to pull donations and funding in I had to create a charity. So, my husband walked with me to the public library where I found many books on the subject, but I had to narrow it down to certain books and plus you could only check out so many.

I began with checking out books on how to create a charity and started there. I checked out five different books and my husband helped me carry them home. I got out my notebook and as I read through the books, I took lots of notes that I would summarize later. There was so much information that my head was swimming in it. I could not believe how many hoops you had to jump through to get a charity started, but I had to start somewhere.

One book after another I read through and took my notes hoping to find an easy way to do this without so much red tape. It took about one and a half notebooks per book of notes to make sure that I had everything needed to start a charity. I was gathering information like I was gathering Easter eggs on a hunt.

My husband left me alone so that I could get all my information uninterrupted. When I was finished with one book, he would take it back to the library. Book after book I searched for information on the basics of setting up a charitable organization that I could use to help the homeless. The thoughts of them being out there weighed heavily on my mind and heart because no human being should have to live like that, and the shelters were full to the max which left a lot of people sleeping outdoors or in abandoned buildings taking the chance of going to jail for trespassing.

My passion to help them kept me going through each of these books gathering the information that I needed. They need my help since I have the experience of being out there and that I know what they are going through. My thoughts and experience are not enough to help them, I needed to get things done in order to proceed in helping them.

After searching and note taking through several books, I now had the information needed to get the basics done. It was going to take a lot of work, but the research wasn't over yet. These books just covered the basic idea and now I had to visit the library again for a new set of books that covered each separate thing that I had to do.

It wasn't just as simple as giving it a name and then registering it with the state. I needed to apply for tax exempt status, come up with bylaws and other forms that would make it legal and impressing to foundations in order to get some funding.

There were several places that I needed to register, apply for an EIN number and a tax-exempt number, among other things which were exhausting mentally. Again, I was back at taking notes from these new books and my husband was concerned if I was taking on too much, but I wasn't. I feel that I was allowed to be homeless for so long so that one day I could go back with the knowledge to help everyone else still out there.

I researched for weeks and then months. It came to a point when my husband and I needed to move, so everything got put on hold for a while so that we could get moved and settled in before I tackled this idea again. We ended up moving to a place where we were in the middle of the city where most of the homeless lived and it pulled at me even more.

Once we got settled in from the move, I jumped right back into researching some more with the couple of books that I had remaining from the library and by this point I had a stack of full notebooks with notes. Once I finished off this set of books, I began going back through my notebooks and prioritizing and summarizing them to where it made sense and in the order of what must be done first.

It truly was exhausting and what kept me going was seeing them every day and visiting some of their camps where they lived. It was horrible to see how they lived and that reignited my passion to finish what I started. I still took trips out with some food and hygiene products to pass out to those who seriously needed them. When I saw panhandlers out and about, I gave them some change from my pocket. If that was all I could do at the time, that was all I could do.

When I finished my notes and had the list of what needed to be done first, I had to wait until I had money to start paying for things. Where my husband and I lived was an old hotel that was turned into some office buildings up front and motel rooms in the back. It was a quiet place to live and it gave me the peace that I needed to keep going over my notes and getting things listed and in place.

REGISTRATION

When the owner of the building found out what I wanted to do, he decided to help me because he was that type of guy who also had a heart and conscience for the homeless. We sat down with my notes and came up with a game plan to get things started. First, he stated that I need to incorporate the name of the charity, which is Hope Station USA, Inc, and we found out the price of that was easy enough for me to purchase, so we did.

While filling out the paperwork online, I had to come up with a mission statement which is in the front of this book. It took me several minutes to think about it before we had the right one. Once all the forms were filled out online, I paid for it and that was it. It seemed so easy and now my charity had a legal name and paperwork to show for it.

After we had everything done with the incorporation, the owner decided to give me an office upstairs in the far corner of the building to run operations. He gave us rent free for a year which was everything I benefits he was not sure he was eligible for and when he got approved, he came back to us in tears that he could now get a place to live instead of behind the mall on the cold concrete.

Those are the moments we cherish when someone comes back to us notifying us that they got a job, or they were approved for food stamps. These are milestones for us that matter because it means they are on the road back to becoming self-sufficient.

Everyone that comes through our door is welcomed with a smile and sometimes a handshake. With some donations coming in food wise, we were able to set up a coffee and pastry bar which was very welcoming to them. They would come in and get some coffee and a pastry and have a seat while waiting their turn. It was a nice touch to the office.

Some individuals came in and asked to speak with me because they knew that I would listen. They just needed someone to listen to their problems and help them with some advice. I would have no problem stopping my work to help them. Most of these individuals just need that ear to hear their cries for help and giving them hope works wonders for their soul and situation.

I have sat and heard women's pleas because of an abusive boyfriend, and they wanted to know how to get out of the relationship or what they should do about it. My life story is told to everyone because then they know I have been there and survived and some want to know my method of how I handled it.

These homeless and needy individuals are people just like you and I and they want someone to listen, to give them advice and some hope that it can be better. My heart goes out to each of them and a lot of the women I have helped get out of the relationships and sent them to the right place for legal issues involving restraining orders.

Our organization has helped and assisted many individuals in gaining employment and securing a safe place of their own to sleep. Many have come back and thanked us for helping them along with the many who have come back and volunteered to help us in our fundraising efforts. We respect them as individuals and human beings.

Society has thrown and tossed them away like trash because all they see is the drugs and alcohol which are the coping mechanisms to hide the guilt and shame that they feel from being out there. They want better for themselves, but some have just been out there so long that it is all they know. They have been institutionalized by the very act and lifestyle of homelessness.

I have seen a lot of them who get their own apartment still live like they are homeless because that is all they know now, and someone needs to help them by teaching them to live like a normal human being. Being taken from the streets and placed into a normal environment can be a scary place for them so people must be patient with some of them, but they all need our help and that hand up.

Most of the individuals out there suffer from mental illness and should be approached cautiously, but they too are still human and should be treated with respect just like any other person in society that accomplish with the program. What do you expect to achieve? List the steps you are going to take to achieve those goals and objectives.

Then, we move on to the methods, strategies, or program design where you walk the grantor through exactly how you plan to use the funding and what steps you will take to achieve your goal. This is where all the fine details of your program or project are explained with a timeline and the who will do what, how, and when. You want to be as specific as you can. Funders like to see that you have thoroughly thought this through.

Next, we come to the section of the grant proposal which is the evaluation part of it. This section will describe what measure's you take to assess your programs accomplishments. Anyone who funds your project or program wants to know that their money did some good and what impact your program made. This is typically showing what records you plan on keeping, what data you collect, and how you use that data.

From here it gets a little easier because now you are at the section of the grant proposal where you inform the funder of any other funding you have received, or that you have asked other sources. Many funders do not want to be the only source of funding for your project, so inform them of any other money coming in and include in-kind donations as well. You also want to inform the funder if this is a short-term project or an ongoing one and if so, how will you sustain it to keep it going? How will it be funded?

The next easiest section would be information about your organization. This can be just a few short paragraphs explaining to the funder that they can trust you to use their funds correctly and efficiently. Be a responsible grantee and make them want to trust you. Give a short history on your organization and what population you serve. State your mission statement and basically just provide them with an overview of your track record. You will also want to list your programs and give them some detail about them.

With all of that done, now you want to create and give them a project budget. This is where you show them the cost of the project and show them expected expenses and income. This will include everything from direct project costs, administrative expenses, and personnel costs. Make it as detailed as possible. You also want to include contributed income in that budget.

As a last part of the grant proposal, you want to include all the additional material that they may need to make an informed decision on your proposal. This usually includes your Internal Revenue Service tax-exempt letter, a list of your board of directors, and a budget for the current fiscal year. There are so many things that go into a good grant proposal.

Now you want to put everything together and include your accompanying documents and mail them out. Now, with more foundations using an online grant application it moves a little quicker than snail mail. It doesn't end there because now you must search out the next foundation that you can submit a grant proposal to and the process starts all over again.

Now you are in a waiting game because most foundations have deadlines for submittal and then you must wait for their next quarterly meeting where they decide to approve you or not. It usually takes about two to four weeks to hear back from them whether they are approving you or not once their meeting is over.

Most of the time you will get more rejections than approvals being a new organization and I know that for a fact. When we first opened and received our tax-exempt status, I spent many long nights writing and putting together grant proposals and waited for months just to get a rejection letter. My advice to those who are thinking about starting a charity, make sure you send out more than one proposal at a time.

I never gave up though. We got a couple one-thousand and five-thousand-dollar checks, but it doesn't last long enough to make a big difference. We started out as a grassroots organization on a very small budget, but I did what I could to keep helping people even when it came out of my own pocket.

No one was being paid for their services and I never got a dime for all the hard work that I did, but it wasn't for a paycheck. I volunteer everyday doing what needs to be done for the organization. We have been incorporated now ten years and we have had a couple bad years due to health and medical conditions which one caused us to lose our Treasurer to lung cancer. She will be missed.

I still have not given up on my organization even after a few bad years. There is still HOPE in me and faith that I can make a change.

I am working back at it with the researching of foundations again and it will be time well spent since I have a passion to help the homeless and compassion for each one of them as an individual.

So, right now we can only get help from the community to continue our efforts in fighting homelessness and poverty until I can get a grant approved to help us. You must do your homework because foundations change what they fund for every year and you need to keep current with it.

My first-year writing grant proposals was a trial and error year. I had so many proposals out I couldn't keep track, but I did because I had a spreadsheet keeping track. You can't just send out one and hope for the best, you need to send out as many as you can, so that while the rejections are coming in hopefully you get approved for one or possibly two.

Getting funding to come in isn't as easy as it may seem. After the office doors closed at five, I stayed in the office sometimes until two o'clock in the morning writing grant proposals and getting them ready to be mailed. Thankfully, today most foundations use the internet for grant application submittals, so you pay less postage, ink, and paper in the long run. There are still those who require the paper form but not as many as you would think.

Fundraising was the easiest part of bringing in money for supplies. We did car washes at different sites and even some street fundraising. I had to go down to the city building to get permits for street fundraising, but it was easy to obtain.

We had volunteers and even some clients come out to help us which showed me how much they appreciated what help we gave them. Usually we had more people show up for fundraising than I knew what to do with.

As far as street fundraising went, I had to purchase neon yellow safety vests and we made buckets out of old plastic coffee cans. I usually put two people on each side of the intersection with more waiting on standby over with a cooler full of water. They would trade out after so long because on an average weekend it was sunny and hot outside.

Another part of fundraising that we did was make appointments to set up a donation table at local stores like Walmart and Walgreens. We would set up our table by the front door and we had pens and brochures to hand out to everyone informing them of who we were and what services we were doing. We did get quite a good response from people about the work we were doing.

Granted we didn't bring in a whole lot of money because we were still new, but it was the fact that we were getting our name out there and bringing awareness of homelessness to everyone. It is a serious issue and it needs to be addressed. We normally had a table set up every weekend at different locations and we had fun sitting there meeting new people and discussing the issue at hand about homelessness. We did meet with adversity at times because society has placed a label on homeless individuals stating, "if they would get a job, they wouldn't be homeless" and sometimes people would be downright rude about it.

We hope here soon to do some more fundraising to bring in funds while I approach the foundations with grant proposals. My health is getting back under control and I am pumped up about tackling society again along with others to bring in funding for new programs that would better assist the homeless in regaining their self-sufficiency.

CHARITY WALKS

After being open for a few months and serving clients, I see that I needed more help. Through word of mouth, I began getting women coming to the office who needed to do so many hours a week for their department of family and children services benefits. I had them in the office helping me with filing paperwork, making up bag lunches and food bags, and serving our clients.

Everything seemed to be going great and clients were being helped and it was all worth it to stand there and see my dream coming true. It was until I started noticing things missing from the office. It was petty things like hygiene products that were for the clients, office supplies, and food. It was a shame that they had to steal when they could have just asked me.

Then, there was another ordeal with community service workers being rude to clients. One, they acted like they didn't want to be there, but then treat a homeless individual like you are better than them is not fair or tolerated. I had to give several warnings to a few of the workers about it until it happened too many more times where I had to make a call and get women placed somewhere else. They were not welcomed back to my organization.

Next, I had people from probation and parole coming to my office to complete their community service hours. They acted a lot better than the women did. They cleaned up around the premises and even did some fundraising events with us. It was a pleasure having them there and getting to know each one on a personal level was interesting.

I never had any problems out them and no one stole from the office. I tried to get people to understand me and how I am, and they caught on quick and gave me respect. A few officers even came by to check us out and were pleased with what we were trying to do, and they also respected me for that.

It finally came to a point where I had to do something noticeable to bring in some funding, so I decided to do a charity walk across America from Orlando, Florida to Los Angeles, California. That took a few months preparing for and phone calls had to be made to set some things up.

I printed up a list of Walmart's all along my would-be path to set up tables for contributions. My Treasurer would set up tables at the locations that accepted us while I did the walking. I closed the office to do the walk because there was no one that I could trust to keep it going.

My Treasurer got ahold of the news reporters and set up interviews all along where I was walking. I started off one morning and began my journey. I did manage to get a lot of attention while walking where people realized who I was and honked their horns in support of what I was trying to do.

I stopped along the way at several establishments to get a drink and restroom breaks and even received donations while I was there. One man driving past me recognized me and almost ran me over trying to stop and get a picture of me. He handed me the last few dollars in his pocket as a donation. He was very appreciative of what I was doing.

The walk was long and hard, but I kept going. I walked even with blisters on my heels because my passion for my journey was more important than those blisters. I walked through most of Florida up the four forty-one highway from Orlando and met a lot of people along the way.

Not only was I walking for the homeless, but I was walking for myself. I was alone on that walk and dealt with a lot of things within me and that made it more worthwhile. I remember being homeless and what it did to me mentally, physically, and emotionally, so I needed that walk just as much as the homeless needed me to walk for them.

At every Walmart we had a table set up, we were always met with adversity and my Treasurer always wanted to know why I held a grudge or got upset at people. I'm not sure what it was myself except for ignorance to the situation. No one seemed to care that human beings were having to live outside like animals mostly.

Humans sleeping on cold concrete, being robbed of what little they did own, and women being raped because they had nowhere to go that was safe. Homeless shelters were at maximum capacity, so where were they to go? These are our family members, neighbors, and friends, but we can't offer them a hand up. That is where Hope Station USA came in, to help.

I walked through Dothan, Alabama, down to New Orleans, and through Louisiana. I noticed that something was wrong with my Treasurer because she was starting to feel pain and ill. We got as far as the Louisiana- Texas border and had to turn back so that she could seek medical help. I could have walked the rest of the way by myself, but no one was going to allow me to do that.

So, we headed back to Orlando, Florida with disappointment in my heart that I could not finish the walk, but my Treasurer's health was more important. Once we were back in Orlando, she tried to get to a doctor, but she had no insurance, and no one would treat her. She fought for a couple years trying to get a diagnosis and treatment but passed away from an aggressive lung cancer. She left behind a five-year-old daughter who is now being raised by her adult sister. She will be missed very much.

It hit me hard emotionally because she was also my best friend who I could share my thoughts and feelings to. It took her a minute to understand why I am mad at society, but she had gotten a first-hand experience during the walk at one of the Walmart tables, when a few people walked out and made snide remarks about the homeless. It really Peeved her off and then she understood.

I didn't reopen Hope Station USA in Orlando because I was still dealing with a few things. I wanted to try another walk, but this one on my own and again, everyone around me would not let me walk alone, but no one could go with me either. They acted like I had never walked around before alone, yet I spent twenty-three years walking around alone and on my own.

Full of disappointment in myself for not making it to the end of my walk, I became homeless again and staying where I could. One of the girls who worked in my office allowed me to move into her house with her, but she failed to tell me that her roommates were using crack cocaine. I tried to stay away from it and began regrouping for Hope Station, but watching people come in and out and all of them using drugs was a threat to my sobriety.

Before I could get Hope Station USA back up and running, I slipped up and used drugs to which my Treasurer had to come rescue me before it got out of hand. I got away from it and my ex-husband at the time allowed me to come stay with him until I could get on my feet again. The only issue with that was his new girlfriend also used drugs and was a prostitute, so staying there was no good either.

I finally found a distant relative who lived here in Georgia and we began talking and I explained my situation to her. She wanted me to move up here with her. I talked to my ex-husband who agreed to move me up here and he instead stayed for a while. I tried to get back on my feet and was working from home as a phone sex worker which made decent money and soon after moving up here, I got a place of my own.

Now, that I had a stable income and a place of my own, it was time to get Hope Station USA back up and running. There were homeless here too and with my research, Atlanta has the highest rate of homeless individuals, so I knew what I had to do. I began my research here and finally had Hope Station registered here in Georgia and kept her registered in Florida as well.

So, now Hope Station USA is registered in both states and I did my best trying to get funding here, but most want to fund for Florida. I stuck with it and even collected food that I stored up in my living room to pass out. My ex-husband came over and we took food down to the streets and fed homeless individuals here in town.

Then, I met my husband who I am still happily married to now and we have put our heads together to come up with ideas to bring in funding. He has gone out with me to pass out food and even bought me a car so that we could be mobile, and Florida can be taken care of as well.

We have done local flea markets to collect donations and I need to make phone calls to Florida to set up tables there to collect donations. It is stressful trying to run two states, but with my know how and experience we can do it. We have a home base here in Georgia and are a mobile unit for Florida.

We should be servicing Florida soon once we get some more funding coming in, but for now, we use our personal money to help those less fortunate. Hope Station USA is considered my baby and I am to nurture her and help her grow. We have been incorporated for ten years now and that should show for something. I will never give up on her.

Hopefully, soon we will also be registering in Tennessee which also has a high homeless rate of individuals. There is a major need for assistance, and everyone should come together to help get them off the streets. They need our help and with support, they can get the addiction help they need and assistance in regaining their self-sufficiency which many of them desire.

With adversity hitting us head on, we seem to struggle but eventually overcome. This year, I plan to do a state walk here in Georgia to raise awareness. I plan on walking through Atlanta and doing a complete circle around the state. I have made an agreement with everyone around me that I will get myself conditioned for this walk and cleared by my doctor.

Once I have finished this walk which my husband is going along with me for support, I plan on doing a state walk of Tennessee in the Spring of next year and a Florida state walk later next year. I want everyone to know the issue at hand and how passionate I am about this walk and the homeless situation. I personally know their struggle and want to help.

While on these walks, I will be keeping a diary on my website to keep everyone up to date on my progress. That is the one thing that we didn't do the first time around, but everything is with trial and error. I will be keeping everyone in the loop with what route I will be walking in case someone wants to give a donation or even just buy me a bottle of water.

This walk should be happening right around the first week of September two-thousand and nineteen. I hope to see the support of our communities and be kept in everyone's thoughts and prayers. I am a forty-eight-year-old woman who is diabetic, but I won't allow that to stop me from seeing this through.

While I am walking, I will be stopping and interviewing homeless individuals and getting their story for another book that I am going to write which should be out in late November. I want society to get to know these people and their story as to how they ended up homeless and what they want out of life.

I am a strong and hard-headed woman when it comes to the homeless and helping them get their life back on the right track. Currently we are working out the details to a program that will be a huge benefit to the homeless and the community. We just need volunteers once we receive funding.

Thank you for reading my book and learning about what our organizations is doing. If you have a spare minute could you please leave a review on the page that you found this book on, or you could forward it to me personally @ brandidpayne.com on the contact page.

<u>Other books that I have written include</u>:

How I Survived Prostitution (1st Book in a series)

Short Stories of Love & Betrayal

The Battle for Joshua

Immortal Passion (1st Book in a series)

Cellarium

Fetish- The Vanilla Side

A percentage of all book royalties will go to Hope Station USA, Inc to support our efforts in assisting the homeless and needy individuals regain their self-sufficiency.

If you would like to show your support and contribute you can at the two links below.

PayPal Fundraising

http://paypal.com/us/fundraiser/charity/1446573

GoFundMe

https://www.gofundme.com/5u9yxn-pathway-to-selfsufficiency